Let's Discover The States

The Northwest

ALASKA • IDAHO • OREGON
WASHINGTON

By
Thomas G. Aylesworth
Virginia L. Aylesworth

CHELSEA HOUSE PUBLISHERS
New York   New Haven   Philadelphia

Sunlight glittering on the snow-capped peaks of the
    Chugach Mountains.
The red glow of the midnight sun at Barrow.
Cries from the crowd as they watch an Eskimo blanket
    toss at an Anchorage festival.
The chugging of a paddlewheeler on the Tanana River.
The glorious color of the fireweed on the banks of the
    Yukon River.
The majesty of the Mendenhall Glacier near Juneau.

Let's Discover
Alaska

★ State Capital
● Cities or towns
■ OF SPECIAL INTEREST

RUSSIA

Penzhin Bay

Chukchi Sea

Barrow ●

Kotzebue Sound

Anadyr Gulf

Bering Strait

● Kotzebue

RUSSIA (U.S.S.R.)
UNITED STATES

Norton Sound

N
△

ALASKA

INTERNATIONAL DATELINE

BERING SEA

Bristol Bay

ALASKA PENINSULA

ALEUTIAN ISLANDS

PACIFIC OCEAN

Distance scale
0 50 100   200   300   400   500   600   700   800   900   1000 Miles
0 50 100 200   300   400   500   600   700   800   900   1000 1100 1200 1300 1400 1500 1600 Kilometres

ALASKA
At a Glance

ARCTIC OCEAN

Amundsen Gulf

NORTHWEST TERRITORIES

CANADA

UNITED STATES

● Fairbanks

— MOUNT MCKINLEY

YUKON

Anchorage
● Spenard

Gulf of Alaska

BRITISH COLUMBIA

MENDENHALL GLACIER ■

★ Juneau

Sitka ●

Ketchikan ●

Capital: Juneau

State Flag

State Bird:
Willow Ptarmigan

State Flower:
Forget-Me-Not

Major Industries: Oil, gas, commercial fishing, tourism

Size: 586,412 square miles (largest)

Population: 500,000 (nation's smallest)

9

The Mendenhall Glacier is an ancient sheet of ice that covers an entire valley. Much of Alaska's rugged terrain is inaccessible to man and has never been fully explored.

The Land

Alaska is located at the northwesternmost part of the North American continent. It is bordered on the west by the Bering Sea, on the north by the Arctic Ocean, on the east by the Canadian Yukon Territory and the province of British Columbia, and on the south by the Pacific Ocean and the Gulf of Alaska. The state has four main land regions: the Pacific Mountain System, the Central Uplands and Lowlands, the Rocky Mountain System, and the Arctic Coastal Plain.

The Pacific Mountain System is a long, narrow region that extends from the Aleutian Islands in the west to the south coast; it is part of a group of mountain ranges that stretch from Alaska to southern California. The area is filled with ice fields and towering peaks, including 20,320-foot Mount McKinley, the highest point in North America. It also has several active volcanoes. The territory includes two areas of lowlands—the Copper River Basin and the Susitna-Cook Inlet Lowland. It is in the Pacific Mountain System that most of the state's industry and farming are situated. Here are dairy farms, grain fields, and coal mines, as well as oil wells and forest-product factories. Fishing is a big industry off the southern coast.

The Central Uplands and Lowlands comprise the largest land area in Alaska and are located just north of the Pacific Mountain System, running east to west. It is a land of low hills and river valleys, where potatoes and grains flourish. Reindeer, introduced from Siberia, are raised here, and the region contains gold, silver, and antimony mines.

The Rocky Mountain system in Alaska consists of the Brooks Range and its foothills, which form a narrow strip running east and west above the Central Uplands and Lowlands. Some natural gas wells are located here.

The Arctic Coastal Plain runs along the northern border of the state. It is a bleak but beautiful land, treeless because the ground is permanently frozen beneath the topsoil. But in the spring the surface soils thaw and are quickly covered with grasses and wildflowers.

Above:
The Alaskan pipeline, which began operations in 1977, transports oil across the state from Prudhoe Bay in the north to Valdez in the south. The discovery in 1968 of huge offshore oil deposits along the Arctic Slope increased Alaska's prosperity dramatically.

At left:
The Matanuska Valley, northeast of Anchorage, is one of the state's most productive farming areas. With a 120-day growing season and summer sunlight of 19 hours, the valley provides about 80 percent of the food supply for nearby Anchorage and other cities and towns.

Above:
The capital city, Juneau, in southeastern Alaska near the British Columbian border, has a dramatic backdrop of mountains. The state's third largest city, Juneau experienced a population increase of 222 percent in the 1970s, largely as a result of the "oil rush."

At right:
Much of Alaska's land is still wild and unsettled. The mountainous terrain makes road-building difficult, and many of the state's resources remain largely untapped. But these same factors make Alaska one of the last great natural wildlife refuges in the world.

The coastline of Alaska is 6,640 miles long. The state has thousands of lakes, and its most important rivers are the Yukon, the Kuskokwim, the Colville, the Tanana, and the Copper.

Just as Alaska varies enormously in topography, so does it vary in climate. Along the southern coasts and the island groups that flank them, the climate is surprisingly mild, thanks to the Japan Current sweeping in from the west. Rainfall is heavy, in places as high as 150 inches per year. The average winter temperatures are about 32 degrees Fahrenheit, with summer temperatures running from 50 to 60 degrees F.

In the southern coastal valleys, in and around Anchorage, it is cooler and drier, with greater extremes both summer and winter—more like the north-central Plains area of the lower 48 states. The island chain to the west has its own peculiar climate—cool and very foggy year round—pleasant only for its native inhabitants, the herds of seals. In the central valley it is still drier, with winter temperatures often falling to 30 or 40 degrees below zero and summer temperatures soaring above 85 degrees F. The average rainfall in the valley regions is only about 15 to 20 inches per year.

Arctic Alaska on the north is, as its name implies, cold most of the time, with a climate comparable to that of northern Norway. But summer days of almost total daylight in various parts of the Arctic warm up the land, encouraging thousands of delicate flowers to bloom.

The History

When Europeans first arrived in what would become Alaska, three different types of native people were living in this vast area: the Eskimos, the Aleuts, and the Indians. The Eskimos lived in the far north and west, generally near the coast, where they hunted sea mammals and fished. Closely related to the Eskimos were the Aleuts, skillful sea hunters who lived on the Aleutian Islands and the Alaska Peninsula. The Alaskan Indians were hunting and fishing people who varied their diet with edible plant materials that were found in the area, as did the other two groups. The Tlingit and the Haida Indians lived along the south coast, which was also inhabited by the less numerous Tsimshian. In the interior were the Athapaskan tribes.

Most people knew nothing about Alaska until other parts of the western hemisphere had been discovered, named, and settled. Alaska's discovery was made almost by accident. In 1725 Czar Peter the Great of Russia commissioned a Danish navigator named Vitus Bering to find out whether North America and Siberia were connected by land. Bering and his men traveled more than 6,000 miles across Russia and Asia to the Siberian coast, where they built a ship, the *Saint Gabriel*, which finally set sail in 1728.

The expedition sailed through what would be named the Bering Strait between Asia and North America, but could not see the Alaskan mainland because of fog. In 1741 Bering made his second voyage, on which he saw Mount Saint Elias in southeastern Alaska and landed on Kayak Island. Shortly thereafter, Bering died of scurvy, a disease resulting from the lack of Vitamin C, which killed many sailors of his time. But members of his party collected animals from the Alaskan coast and took them back to Russia. They included the sea otter and the fur seal.

Furs were important to Russia, and the pelts brought to the imperial court by Bering's men were among the sleekest, softest, and

English captain James Cook explored and mapped the Alaskan coastline in 1778, six years before the Russians made their settlement on Kodiak Island. During the early 1800s, there was fierce rivalry between fur traders from Russia and the British Hudson's Bay Company. The coastal waters were rich with otter, seal, and other fur-bearing animals, which led to constant boundary disputes.

richest ever seen. So hunters and trappers from Siberia, called *promyshlenniki*, crossed the fog-swept channel that separated Alaska from Siberia and began to slaughter the seals and sea otters. The wealth of furs in Alaska was so great that large Russian companies were formed to exploit it. One of them was responsible for the first European settlement in Alaska, on Kodiak Island, just off the southwest coast, in 1784. Then the Russian government took an official interest and formed the Russian-American Company in 1799. Alexander Baranof was its manager, and he selected a site near present-day Sitka as his headquarters. This company was the only governing power in Alaska for the next 68 years.

Baranof treated the Indians ruthlessly and made slaves of the Aleuts. In 1802 the Tlingit Indians revolted, attacking Sitka and massacring many Russian settlers. The town was rebuilt in 1804, and it remains the most Russian-looking city in North America. From Sitka, the Russian colonists extended their claims and control as far south as California.

Baranof died in 1819, and thereafter Russian interest in Alaska declined. In 1823 the young United States of America proclaimed the Monroe Doctrine, opposing further European colonization or influence in North America, which was aimed in part at the Russian hold on the Northwest. Britain and the United States agreed on zones of influence that limited Russia still more.

While Russia's interest in, and profits from, Alaska diminished, those of the United States increased. The West Coast fishing interests wanted control of Alaskan waters. The Western Union Telegraph Company had a plan to lay a cable to Siberia, and thence to Europe, by way of Alaska. Toward the middle of the 19th century, Russia began to liquidate its North American domain, first selling its California holdings and claims to a Swiss immigrant named John Sutter (it was on his property that gold was discovered in 1848).

International trends came to a climax in 1867, when William H. Seward, the United States Secretary of State in the Andrew Johnson administration, offered Russia $7.2 million for Alaska. The deal was made within a matter of hours (actually, Russia wanted out so badly that it would have settled for $5 million) and was signed at 4:00 A.M. on March 30, 1867. Opponents of the Alaska Purchase labeled it "Seward's Folly," "Seward's Icebox," and "Johnson's Polar Bear Garden."

The American flag went up over Sitka on October 18, 1867, and the entire vast new land was put in charge of a few U.S. Army officers. Then, in 1880, gold was discovered near what is now Juneau, resulting in a small stampede of prospectors. Ironically, it was not this discovery, but rather gold strikes in the Klondike region of Canada to the east, in 1896, that caused the famous rush to Alaska.

U.S. Secretary of State William H. Seward was instrumental in purchasing Alaska from Russia. Seward and his eloquent colleague Charles Sumner endorsed the chance to buy the huge area for $7,200,000—less than two cents per acre. The sale was consummated on March 30, 1867, after months of sharp debate and Congressional opposition. Alaska was referred to at the time as "Seward's Ice Box" and "Seward's Folly."

Sitka was an important commercial center in Russian Alaska at the turn of the 19th century. Founded in 1799 by Siberian merchant Alexander Baranof, it was headquarters for the Russian-American Company, which exploited Alaska's native peoples and wildlife to advance its fur-trading interests.

It was easier to reach the Klondike by way of Alaska than across the rugged wilds of Canada. Some of the prospectors returning from the Canadian Yukon joined the Nome Rush in 1899 and the rush near Fairbanks in 1903. These miners, called sourdoughs for the bread they baked from fermented dough, made headlines all over the world. Few of them made much money from gold, but they created robust and colorful legends. Young writers like Robert Service, Jack London, and Rex Beach made more money recording the exploits of the sourdoughs than most miners made from their claims.

The era of modern Alaska officially began in 1912, with the establishment of local government, preceded by relocation of the capital from Sitka to Juneau in 1906. The hysteria of individual gold prospecting was over. Gold mining had become big business, conducted by great placer mines and dredging. Fishing became more important. Lumber interests began to use the timber from the forests. The Alaskan Railway from Seward to Fairbanks was begun in 1915.

The entry of the United States into World War II in 1941 gave enormous impetus to Alaskan air travel, both civil and military, particularly long-range intercontinental flights. Alaska became the center for shorter routes between the United States and the Orient and Europe. The territory also became the first line of domestic defense. Army camps, naval bases, and air bases sprang up. The 1,500-mile Alaska Highway was built to provide a land link. Thousands of young men, and many of their families, went to Alaska to help install and man the new bases. Engineers and lumbermen discovered that Alaska was incredibly rich in natural resources, including mineral wealth and timber.

In June of 1942, Japanese amphibious forces landed on Agattu, Attu, and Kiska, in the westernmost Aleutians. The following March a U.S. naval force defeated the Japanese off the western Aleutians in the first battle fought in American territory since that of Appomattox, at the end of the Civil War. Of more than 300,000 military personnel stationed in the area during the war, many stayed, or returned as civilian citizens.

On January 3, 1959, Alaska became the 49th state of the Union, with William Egan as its first governor. Ernest Gruening and Edward Lewis "Bob" Bartlett were elected U.S. senators and Ralph J. Rivers became the U.S. representative.

In 1977 the vast trans-Alaska pipeline was completed. Extending for 800 miles, it is designed to carry one and a half million barrels of oil a day from the Arctic shore to the southern port of Valdez.

Today, Alaska still has problems in trying to develop its huge land area with a very sparse and widely scattered population. The expenses of transportation and shipping make the cost of living extremely high, and roads and railroads are difficult to build because of the mountains. But Alaska's hardy people are well suited to the task of developing their wild and beautiful state, which is truly the nation's last frontier.

In addition to the regular public-school systems in the state of Alaska, the United States Bureau of Indian Affairs operates schools for native children in many Eskimo, Aleut, Tlingit, Haida, and Athapaskan villages. The first institution of higher education in the state was the University of Alaska, which was founded in 1917—42 years before Alaska joined the Union.

Alaskan Indian culture thrives in the southwest corner of the state. Here, members of the Tlingit tribe prepare for a ritual dance in traditional dress. The culture of these Indians, similar to tribes in nearby Canada, is distinctive to the northwest coast of North America.

The People

More than 64 percent of the people in Alaska live in cities and towns, the largest of which are Anchorage and Fairbanks; only about one-third of them were born in the state. Most of those from outside the state are members of the U.S. armed forces stationed in this strategic area where North America, Asia, and Europe are in close proximity to one another. The largest religious groups in Alaska are the Roman Catholic, Russian Orthodox, and Protestant communities, including the Baptist, Presbyterian, Methodist, Episcopal, and Lutheran Churches.

Alaska's native peoples are the Eskimos, the Aleuts, the Northwest Coast Indians such as the Tlingit and Haida tribes, and several Athapaskan tribes.

The Eskimos have no tribal groups as such, but they are similarly organized into linguistic and community groups. The family is their primary social unit, and community rules of conduct take the place of strict legal systems among them. Their traditional way of life revolves around the search for food, especially sea animals. The Eskimos have contributed the words igloo, kayak, and parka to the English language, and they are skilled carvers of small objects in bone, ivory, and soapstone. The Northwest Coast Indians of Alaska are expert carvers of wood and stone. Their colorful totem poles and "spirit houses," which ornament their cemeteries, are striking features of the Alaskan landscape. They are also renowned boat builders, weavers, and fishermen.

Alaska's pioneering politicians include William Egan, the state's first governor, and Bob Bartlett, Ralph J. Rivers, and Ernest Gruening, its first members of Congress. Prospector Joe Juneau, of the 1880 gold rush, typified the venturesome spirit of Alaska's frontier days and gave his name to the state capital. Other pioneers included refugees from the Dust Bowl of the Depression era, who made the Matanuska Valley, near Anchorage, the center of Alaskan agriculture. In recent years the "oil rush" has attracted new residents into the 49th state.

At left:
Eskimos were living in Alaska thousands of years before European explorers arrived. Today, the state's population includes more than 65,000 Indians, Eskimos, and Aleuts.

At right:
A wooden mask, *The Mouse Man*, from Tlingit, Alaska.

Below:
A rattle, made of wood in the shape of a raven, from Haida, Alaska.

The governor's mansion in Juneau.

OF SPECIAL INTEREST

ON THE ARCTIC COAST: *Eskimo Villages*
In these villages the people follow their ancestral ways of life—ice fishing, caribou hunting, and going to sea in kayaks for seal and walrus.

IN SOUTH-CENTRAL ALASKA: *Mount McKinley National Park*
This scenic preserve in the Alaska Range is named for majestic Mount McKinley, which rises 20,320 feet to the highest elevation in North America.

IN ANCHORAGE: *The Anchorage Fur Rendezvous Festival*
Held for a week in February, it features sled-dog races, Eskimo blanket tosses, athletic contests, and other entertainment.

IN SOUTHEASTERN ALASKA: *Glacier Bay National Monument*
Some 2 million acres of awe-inspiring wilderness include the mile-wide Muir Glacier. Glacier Bay is a major attraction of Alaska's Inside Passage between the mainland and the open sea.

NEAR JUNEAU: *Mendenhall Glacier*
This ancient ice sheet fills an entire valley with ice and stone.

For more information write:
ALASKA CHAMBER OF COMMERCE
310 SECOND STREET
JUNEAU, ALASKA 99801

FURTHER READING

Alaska: High Roads to Adventure. National Geographic Society, 1976.
Carpenter, Allan. *Alaska*, rev. ed. Childrens Press, 1979.
Fradin, Dennis B. *Alaska in Words and Pictures.* Childrens Press, 1977.
Hunt, William R. *Alaska: A Bicentennial History.* Norton, 1976.
Naske, Claus-Michael, and Slotnick, S.E. *Alaska: A History of the 49th State.* Eerdmans, 1979.
Wheeler, Keith. *The Alaskans.* Time, Inc., 1977.

Colorfully clad skiers on the snow-covered slopes at
  Sun Valley.
The peaks of the Sawtooth Mountains rising above
  beautiful meadows.
Shepherds of Basque descent watching their flocks.
The thrills of the Frontier Rodeo in Pocatello.
A rainbow rising from the mists at Shoshone Falls near
  Twin Falls.
The time-worn Cataldo Mission near Kellogg—the
  oldest building in the state.

Let's Discover
Idaho

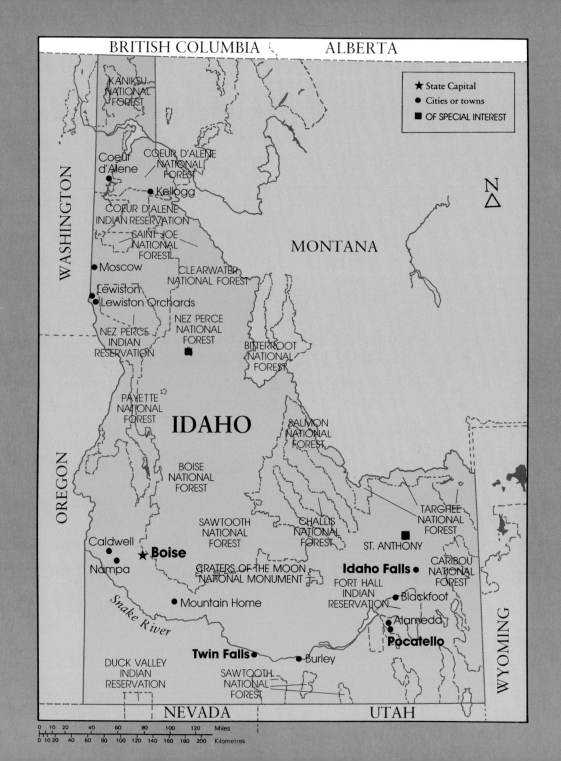

IDAHO
At a Glance

Capital: Boise

Major Industries: Agriculture, livestock, lumbering, mining, electronics

State Flower: Syringa

Size: 83,557 square miles (13th largest)
Population: 1,001,000 (40th largest)

State Bird:
Mountain Bluebird

State Flag

Above:
At Shoshone Falls, in southern Idaho, the Snake River tumbles 212 feet over a sheer cliff to form one of the nation's greatest waterfalls.

Above right:
The mighty Snake River, more than 1,000 miles long, flows west across southern Idaho and then north to become part of the state's western border. Between Idaho and Oregon, it slashes through the rock of Hells Canyon to create the deepest cut on the North American continent.

The Land

The shape of Idaho is curious. The southern part is a rectangle 310 miles east to west, 175 miles north to south. But the upper part is a narrowing panhandle only 45 miles wide at the northern end, where it abuts the Canadian province of British Columbia. The western border, divided between Washington and Oregon, is 483 miles north to south. South of the ruler-straight southern border are the states of Nevada and Utah. In the east, the winding state line is shared with Wyoming and Montana. Idaho has three major land regions: the Rocky Mountains Region, the Columbia Plateau, and the Basin and Range Region.

The Rocky Mountains Region is Idaho's largest, covering the panhandle, forming a bow down three-quarters of the state, and on the east forming a strip along the Wyoming border. This region includes some of the most rugged areas in the United States. Parts of it can be explored only on foot or on horseback. Plateaus, valleys, mountains, canyons, and gorges typify this area. In the valleys there are wheat and pea farms, with some hog and beef ranches. It is a land of natural resources, where forest products are harvested and gold, copper, zinc, lead, thorium, mercury, uranium, and silver are mined.

The Columbia Plateau runs parallel to the Snake River in southern Idaho, then curves north along the western border. It has fertile valleys where sugar beets, potatoes, alfalfa, beans, and other crops are grown on irrigated land. This is also a region of cattle and sheep ranches.

The Basin and Range Region is in the southeastern part of the state. Its mountains alternate with deep valleys and grassy plains. Cattle, sheep, and wheat are raised here.

Idaho has more than 50 mountains that rise higher than 10,000 feet above sea level. The highest mountain in the state, Borah Peak, reaches 12,662 feet. Idaho's most important rivers are the Snake, the Salmon, the Columbia, the Kootenai, and the Spokane. There are mineral springs in Idaho, and many spectacular waterfalls. Idaho has more than 2,000 explored lakes, but geographers estimate that there are hundreds more that have not been discovered.

Idaho's climate is of the dry continental type, quite cold in winter, often very hot in summer. Lack of humidity, and prevailing west winds from the Pacific Ocean, give the most populated areas an ideal four-season climate. Annual rainfall ranges from 8 to 20 inches, and winter snowfall in the mountains varies from 40 to 100 inches.

Below left:
Bogus Basin, in southeastern Idaho, forms a dramatic snow-covered landscape. The state's mountainous terrain has made it a favorite with skiers. Sun Valley, in the Sawtooth Mountains, is an internationally famous resort.

Below:
Idaho potatoes, famous for their outstanding flavor, are the state's best-known crop. By the early 1980s, Idaho was producing more than a quarter of all the potatoes grown in the United States.

The History

There were people living in what would become Idaho more than 10,000 years ago. These Paleo-Indians are known through archeological finds, including paintings and carving on rocks, called petroglyphs. When Canadians and Americans arrived, they found members of the Nez Percé, Coeur d'Alene, Pend d'Oreille, Shoshone, Kutenai, and Bannock tribes. The wilderness teemed with fur-bearing animals, fish, and game.

Meriwether Lewis and William Clark were probably the first non-Indians to explore the Idaho region, during their expedition through the lands of the Louisiana Purchase. They crossed the huge Bitterroot Range in 1805 and floated down the Clearwater and Snake Rivers to the west's greatest river, the Columbia. Their reports of innumerable fur-bearing animals brought the trappers, and in 1809 a Canadian explorer, David Thompson, set up a trading post at Pend Oreille Lake. Later, in 1834, Fort Boise and Fort Hall were built to compete against each other for the fur trade.

The first white settlers in Idaho were two Presbyterian missionaries, Henry H. Spalding and his wife. They organized the Lapwai Mission Station, near present-day Lewiston, in 1836. In 1855 a group of Mormons began farming in the eastern part of the area and built Fort Lemhi, but they were forced out by Indian

Below:
Covered wagons were the primary means of transportation for pioneers who settled the Northwest. Many traveled the rugged Oregon Trail, which ran across southern Idaho.

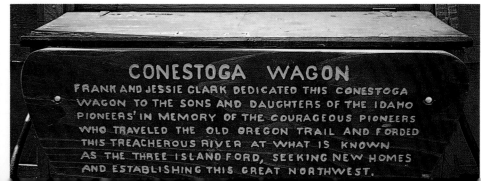

CONESTOGA WAGON
FRANK AND JESSIE CLARK DEDICATED THIS CONESTOGA WAGON TO THE SONS AND DAUGHTERS OF THE IDAHO PIONEERS' IN MEMORY OF THE COURAGEOUS PIONEERS WHO TRAVELED THE OLD OREGON TRAIL AND FORDED THIS TREACHEROUS RIVER AT WHAT IS KNOWN AS THE THREE ISLAND FORD, SEEKING NEW HOMES AND ESTABLISHING THIS GREAT NORTHWEST.

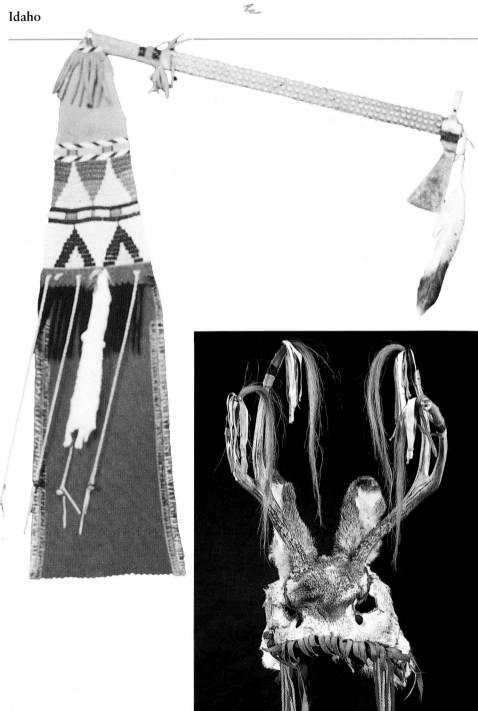

At left:
A Shoshone tomahawk, decorated with beadwork and feathers.

Below left:
The Shoshone Indians were among the first inhabitants of the Idaho region. Their clothing, elaborate headdresses, and other accessories were made from the skins, bones, feathers, and fur of the animals that were found in the area.

Chief Joseph led his people in the Nez Percé War of 1877, when the federal government attempted to settle them on Idaho's Lapwai Reservation from their Oregon lands in the Wallowa Valley. Joseph and his followers won the Battle of White Bird Canyon in north-central Idaho, then conducted a fighting retreat toward the Canadian border against superior government forces. In October 1877, they were finally forced to surrender, and Joseph, moved by his people's suffering, vowed, "I will fight no more forever."

attacks. In 1860 a new party of Mormons arrived and founded Idaho's first permanent white settlement at Franklin.

Most Americans paid little attention to remote Idaho until gold was discovered on Orofino Creek in the Clearwater country in 1860, followed by rich strikes in the Salmon River and Florence areas, the Boise Basin, and Coeur d'Alene. Gold seekers poured into the Idaho region, but after the mines had been exhausted, the gold camps became ghost towns. Farmers and ranchers, however, had come to the area to feed the miners, and the agriculture and livestock industries had begun.

In 1863 the Idaho Territory was established, with Lewiston as its capital. This territory included present-day Idaho, Montana, and almost all of Wyoming. Later, Montana (in 1864) and Wyoming (in 1868) became separate territories. The capital of the Idaho Territory was moved to Boise in 1864.

The 1870s brought fierce Indian wars to Idaho. In 1877 the Nez Percé War broke out when the United States Army tried to force this tribe to move onto the Lapwai Reservation in Idaho. Under the leadership of Chief Joseph, the Nez Percé revolted, crushing army troops in a battle at White Bird Canyon in north-central Idaho on June 17. But the Indians were forced to retreat when more U.S. soldiers were brought into action. Chief Joseph surrendered in October 1877 near the Canadian border.

The Bannock Indians rebelled in 1877 and 1878, because food was scarce on their reservation and they had lost their traditional hunting grounds to settlers. When they began to dig roots for food from the prairie, the cattle ranchers objected and the army was called in. A war broke out, but when the Bannock chief Buffalo Horn was killed, the Indians surrendered.

It was in 1890 that Idaho entered the Union as the 43rd state. Still, it wasn't until the end of the 19th century that the trickle of settlers became a steady flow. Rich silver and lead deposits were found, and a railroad managed to thread the mountain gorges and tunnel through the peaks.

Sheep raising became an important agricultural product in Idaho in the years leading up to World War I.

During the 1890s violence erupted between the miners and mine owners, and between union and nonunion miners. The Coeur d'Alene region was the scene of dynamiting and shooting until the U.S. Army was called in to enforce a peace. In the years that followed, lumbering and sheep raising became more widespread. The volcanic soil of the Snake River Valley in the south was good for crops, and extensive farming, aided by irrigation, began.

When the United States entered World War I in 1917, Idaho's agriculture began to boom. But the state's farmers tended to overexpand, and after the war, while the rest of the country enjoyed prosperity, they were in debt and hard pressed to make a living. Then, oddly enough, recovery began during the Great Depression of the 1930s, when farmers moved in from the drought-ridden Great Plains, having discovered that Idaho's farmlands were still productive.

World War II brought more boom times to the state. Idaho's agricultural products were in great demand, and state factories made arms, munitions, and airplanes. After the war, the national housing boom spurred Idaho's lumber industry. The first nuclear reactors for generating electricity by atomic energy were built in Arco in the 1950s.

Today, the population of Idaho is shifting from rural areas to cities and towns, as the state becomes more industrialized and diversified. The lumber industry, for example, is now manufacturing such wood and paper products as prefabricated houses, boxes, paper cups, and other items. Tourism has become an important source of revenue. Improved transportation has made Idaho more accessible and opened up new markets for its products.

When Idaho became a state, 1,280 acres in each township were set aside for the support of schools. The first institution of higher education in Idaho was the University of Idaho, established in 1889, one year before statehood. This was followed by the College of Idaho in 1891.

The People

Some 54 percent of the people in Idaho live in towns and cities, the largest of which are Boise and Pocatello. Most of them are descendants of early English, Irish, and Scottish settlers from the Eastern and Midwestern states, but Japanese, Scandinavians, Germans, Spaniards from the Basque province, and Canadians are also represented. The Mormons are the largest single religious group in the state. Other major denominations include the Roman Catholic, Methodist, Lutheran, Episcopalian, and Presbyterian.

Sacagawea, the Shoshone Indian woman who served as guide and interpreter to the Lewis and Clark expedition, was born in what is now Idaho. William E. Borah, a native of Illinois, had a distinguished career in Idaho politics as a prosecutor of the mine workers who assassinated Governor Frank Steunenberg after the violent labor conflicts of the 1890s. He also served as a Republican senator from Idaho and in 1922 introduced a resolution to outlaw war; he remained a pacifist even after the United States entered World War II in 1941. Another famous resident of Idaho was Gutzon Borglum, who sculpted the monumental heads of four presidents on Mount Rushmore. Borglum was born near Bear Lake.

Craters of the Moon
National Monument.

OF SPECIAL INTEREST

NEAR KELLOGG: *Cataldo Mission*
Begun in the 1840s by Father Anthony Ravalli, a Catholic missionary, and his
    Indian converts, Idaho's oldest building is now an historic site.

SOUTH OF LEWISTON: *Hells Canyon*
The deepest canyon in the United States, descending at one point to 7,900 feet, is
    on the Snake River.

NEAR TWIN FALLS: *Shoshone Falls*
A beautiful waterfall plunges over 200 feet into the Snake River Canyon.

NEAR ARCO: *Craters of the Moon National Monument*
This rugged region is dotted with craters formed by volcanic activity several
    thousand years ago. It resembles the surface of the moon as seen through a
    telescope.

NEAR ST. ANTHONY: *Crystal Falls Cave*
This ice cave contains a frozen river, a frozen waterfall, and other beautiful
    formations of ice and stone.

For more information write:
THE DIVISION OF ECONOMIC AND COMMUNITY AFFAIRS
STATE CAPITOL BUILDING
BOISE, IDAHO 83720

FURTHER READING

Carpenter, Allan. *Idaho*, rev. ed. Childrens Press, 1979.
Fradin, Dennis B. *Idaho in Words and Pictures*. Childrens Press, 1980.
Idaho: A Guide in Word and Picture, 2nd rev. ed. Oxford, 1950.
Jensen, Dwight W. *Discovering Idaho: A History*. Caxton, 1977.
Peterson, Frank Ross. *Idaho: A Bicentennial History*. Norton, 1976.
Young, Virgil M. *The Story of Idaho*. University Press of Idaho, 1977.

Sunset on the Pacific coast at Cannon Beach.

An aerial view of Portland with snow-crowned Mount Hood rising in the distance.

Branding time on a cattle ranch near John Day.

Lumberjacks guiding logs to a sawmill along a wide river.

The action-packed festivities of the Timber Carnival at Albany.

The peaceful, stately beauty of magnificent Crater Lake in the Cascade Mountains.

Let's Discover
Oregon

WASHINGTON

★ State Capital
● Cities or towns
■ OF SPECIAL INTEREST

Astoria

Saint Helens

The Dalles

Forest Grove
Portland ● Gresham

SIUSLAW
NATIONAL
FOREST

MOUNT HOOD
NATIONAL
FOREST

Dallas ● ★ **Salem**

WARM SPRINGS
INDIAN
RESERVATION

Newport

PACIFIC OCEAN

● Corvallis

OCHOCO
NATIONAL
FOREST

SIUSLAW
NATIONAL
FOREST

WILLAMETTE
NATIONAL
FOREST

● **Eugene**

● Bend

OCHOCO
NATIONAL
FOREST

Cottage Grove

DESCHUTES
NATIONAL
FOREST

North Bend
Coos Bay

UMPQUA
NATIONAL
FOREST

WINEMA
NATIONAL
FOREST

● Barnes
Roseburg ●

CRATER LAKE
NATIONAL PARK

N
△

ROGUE RIVER
NATIONAL
FOREST

FREMONT
NATIONAL
FOREST

SISKIYOU
NATIONAL
FOREST

● Grants Pass

Medford ●

OREGON CAVES
NATIONAL
■ MONUMENT

● Ashland

Klamath Falls
● Altamont

FREMONT
NATIONAL
FOREST

CALIFORNIA

0	10	20		40		60		80		100		120		Miles

0	10	20	40	60	80	100	120	140	160	180	200	Kilometres

Map

- Hermiston
- Pendleton
- UMATILLA NATIONAL FOREST
- UMATILLA INDIAN RESERVATION
- La Grande
- WALLOWA-WHITMAN NATIONAL FOREST
- UMATILLA NATIONAL FOREST
- UMATILLA NATIONAL FOREST
- Baker
- WALLOWA-WHITMAN NATIONAL FOREST
- PICTURE GORGE
- MALHEUR NATIONAL FOREST
- Ontario
- IDAHO

OREGON

- HART MOUNTAIN NATIONAL ANTELOPE REFUGE
- FORT MCDERMITT INDIAN RESERVATION

NEVADA

OREGON
At a Glance

Capital: Salem

State Flag:

State Bird:
Western Meadowlark

State Flower:
Oregon Grape

Major Industries: Forest products, machinery, agriculture, livestock

Size: 96,981 square miles (10th largest)

Population: 2,674,000 (30th largest)

Above:
Smith Rock State Park is typical of the rough terrain in much of central Oregon, where ancient volcanic activity created dramatic peaks and valleys.

Below:
Winchester Bay is on the state's Pacific coast, which offers great scenic variety. The Oregon shoreline ranges from wide beaches and sand dunes to sheer rocky cliffs that rise abruptly from the sea.

The Land

Oregon is bounded on the west by the Pacific Ocean, on the north by Washington, on the east by Idaho, and on the south by California and Nevada. The state has six main land regions, which are the Coast Range, the Willamette Lowland, the Cascade Mountains, the Klamath Mountains, the Columbia Plateau, and the Basin and Range Region.

The Coast Range runs along the Pacific coast from the northwest corner of the state to the Klamath Mountains in the southwest. This is an area of low mountain ranges and evergreen forests. There are several valleys in the region, and along much of the coast, sheer cliffs rise from the ocean. It is an area of fruit and walnut orchards, dairy and poultry farms, and lumbering operations.

The Willamette Lowland is a narrow strip east of the Coast Range, running about halfway down the state. This is a region of gently rolling farmland with many forests. Rich soil and a favorable climate make it the most important farming area in Oregon, and good water transportation facilities make it the state's most important manufacturing region as well.

The Cascade Mountains dominate a broad belt of rugged land with their volcanic peaks, which run from Canada into northern California. Mount Hood, the highest peak in Oregon—11,245 feet above sea level—is in the Cascades.

The Klamath Mountains are in the southwestern corner of Oregon. Thick forests clothe the mountainsides and many game animals live here. Farms and sheep ranches are common in the area, which is also rich in mineral resources such as nickel.

The Columbia Plateau covers most of eastern Oregon and extends into Washington and Idaho. This is where Oregon's vast wheat fields are located. There are also mountains in the region, as well as huge forests and deep canyons. Much of the land has been made productive by irrigation.

Above:
Eastern Oregon has much of the state's flat, open land, on which cattle and wheat are raised.

At left:
Mount Hood, in the Cascade Mountains, is the state's highest peak. The Cascade Range extends from northern to southern Oregon, with many elevations of 10,000 feet or more.

The Basin and Range Region covers part of southeastern Oregon and extends into California and other nearby states. This is mainly a high basin with few mountains, but the Cascade Range to the west cuts off moisture-bearing winds from the ocean and turns this territory into a semi-desert, suitable mainly for sheep and cattle ranching.

Oregon has a coastline of 296 miles, and much of the shore is quite rugged. The most important rivers in Oregon are the Columbia, the Willamette, and the Snake. There are many great lakes in Oregon, especially in the Cascade Mountains. The most famous is Crater Lake, 1,932 feet deep, which is the deepest lake in the United States. It was formed in the basin of an extinct volcano.

Along the coast, Oregon's climate is mild and moist, due in part to warm ocean currents. Rainfall, most common in the fall and winter, is about 75 inches per year. Portland, some 100 miles from the coast, has average January temperatures of about 38 degrees Fahrenheit, and average summer temperatures of only 67 degrees F. In the eastern half of the state, beyond the Cascade Range, the climate is so dry that average rainfall amounts to only a little more than 10 inches per year, and summers are generally hot.

Below right:
The Basin and Range Region, in southeast Oregon, is generally rocky and dry. The Cascade Mountains to the west cut off moisture-bearing winds from the Pacific Ocean.

Below:
Many of Oregon's lakes are in the central region, where drainage from the Cascade and Blue Mountains provides an abundant water supply.

The Lewis and Clark expedition was one of the first to explore the Oregon Territory. They employed the services of an Indian woman, Sacagawea, to act as interpreter for the group.

The History

There were many Indian tribes living in the Oregon territory when the first Europeans arrived. The Chinook fished for salmon along the lower Columbia River. In the northwest lived the Clackama, the Multnomah, and the Tillamook. East of the Cascade Range were the Bannock, the Cayuse, the Paiute, the Umatilla, and a branch of the Nez Percé. Along what is now the boundary between Oregon and California lived the Klamath and the Modoc.

Though the coast of Oregon was sighted and mentioned by Spanish navigators who went from Mexico to the Philippines in the 16th century, no one took much interest in it for quite a few years.

Some historians think that the English sea captain Sir Francis Drake may have touched on the Oregon southern coast in 1579 while searching for a route from the Northern Pacific to the Atlantic. Another British explorer, James Cook, discovered and named Cape Foulweather, north of Yaquina Bay, in 1778.

But Oregon attracted little attention until an American named Robert Gray sailed into and named the Columbia River in 1792. Soon after that, Meriwether Lewis and William Clark made the region famous with their report of its wealth and wonders. While on their exploratory trip through the Louisiana Purchase in 1805, they pioneered the route that would become the Oregon Trail, and their explorations, along with Gray's, gave the United States a strong claim to the Oregon territory.

In the early 1800s the Oregon region extended from Alaska (claimed by Russia) to California (claimed by Spain). East and west, it stretched from the Pacific to the Rocky Mountains. The fur trader John Jacob Astor created an American presence in Oregon when he built his trading post at Astoria in 1811. But he was frightened into selling it to the British North West Company during the War of 1812. Both the British and the Russians maintained their claims to Oregon.

In 1834 the first permanent American settlement was established by Methodist missionaries in the Willamette Valley. But population grew slowly, chiefly by way of wagon trains that had plodded across the mountains and prairie lands. Settlers were intent on building homes in forest clearings and farming the rich valleys. Many came from New England and gave such names as Portland, Salem, Medford, Albany, and Newport to their communities. Others were from the Middle West. In 1843 the region was proved accessible when a great wagon train led by Dr. Elijah White followed the Oregon Trail that began in Missouri.

From then on, hundreds of American settlers began arriving, and the United States government was motivated to settle its boundary disputes with Great Britain (Russia had given up its claims). In 1846

Fur trader John Jacob Astor established the post of Astoria in 1811. During the War of 1812, it was seized by the British, but Astor's American Fur Company set up other outposts that dominated the trade. Astor helped create a significant American presence in Oregon, where four nations—Russia, Spain, Great Britain, and the United States—were pressing their claims to the region.

the two countries agreed on the present dividing line of the 49th parallel as the boundary between the United States and Canada.

The Indian wars in Oregon—which were largely the result of treaty violations and excessive military force on the part of the United States government—began with the massacre of missionary Marcus Whitman and 11 others near Walla Walla (now in Washington) in 1847. This was followed by the Cayuse War of 1847, the Rogue River Wars of the 1850s, the Modoc War of 1872–73, the Nez Percé War of 1877, and the Paiute and Bannock Uprisings of 1878. Not until 1890 were the Indian wars effectively ended throughout the West.

In 1848 Oregon had become a territory, with its capital at Oregon City. The capital was moved to Salem in 1850. In 1855 Congress carved the Washington Territory out of the Oregon Territory, and in 1859, Oregon joined the Union as the 33rd state. Later the railroads linked it to the East, and the rate of settlement increased—farms, forests, fish, and furs were the attractions.

After the Civil War, veterans from both sides began arriving in Oregon to seek new opportunities. The population of the state increased sixfold in a mere 30 years. Women were given the right to vote and hold office in 1912.

During World War I, an astonishing 44,000 Oregonians served in the armed forces. Oregon became a "war-boom" state during World War II. Factories were producing military equipment; Portland became a major port from which this equipment was shipped to troops in the Pacific Theater; cargo vessels and warships were built.

Today, Oregon is on the move. Increased irrigation has opened vast new areas of farmland. Hydroelectric plants on the Columbia and Willamette River systems provide power that encourages industrial growth. The tourist industry is booming as a result of Oregon's many natural attractions and opportunities for outdoor sports, camping, boating, and other recreational activities.

The first school in Oregon was established by a Methodist missionary, Jason Lee, at French Prairie in 1834. A free public-school system was mandated by law in 1849. By the time that Oregon became a state in 1859, it had four institutions of higher education: Willamette University (1842), Linfield College (1849), Pacific University (1849), and Oregon College of Education (1856). By the turn of the century, seven more had been established—Lewis and Clark College (1867), Oregon State University (1868), the University of Oregon (1872), Mount Angel College (1887), Mount Angel Seminary (1889), George Fox College (1892), and Northwest Christian College (1895). Oregon's first circulating library opened in Oregon City in 1842.

Strawberry pickers work productive fields in northern Oregon, near Mount Hood.

The People

Almost 68 percent of the people in Oregon live in cities and towns—many of them in the Willamette Valley in such cities as Portland and Salem. About 96 percent of Oregonians were born in the United States, many of them tracing their ancestry back to settlers who came in on the Oregon Trail. Of those born in other nations, most came from Canada and the Scandinavian countries. The majority of Oregon's churchgoers are Protestants—Baptists, Disciples of Christ, Episcopalians, Lutherans, Methodists, Mormons, and Presbyterians. But the largest single religious body consists of Roman Catholics.

One of the most impressive figures in Oregon history was Chief Joseph of the Nez Percé, who made a courageous but hopeless stand against government seizure of his people's lands in the Wallowa Valley. Another distinguished native of Oregon was Linus Pauling, one of the few people in history to win two Nobel Prizes. His feat was all the more astonishing because he first won the prize in chemistry (1954) and then received the Nobel Peace Prize (1962). Pauling was born in Portland. Edwin Markham, born in Oregon City, was a renowned poet best known for "The Man with the Hoe." CBS sports anchorman Brent Musberger is a native of Portland.

Oregon's mountain ranges, rivers, lakes, and state parks provide many recreational opportunities. Green Lakes Basin, in Deschutes County, is one of the state's most popular hiking areas.

The breathtaking Wallowa Mountains are closely tied to Oregon's Indian heritage.

OF SPECIAL INTEREST

IN SALEM: *State Capitol*
Constructed of marble in modernized Greek style, this impressive state house has a cylinder-shaped dome topped by a golden statue, *Pioneer*, and monuments to the men and women who opened Oregon to settlement.

IN PORTLAND: *Pittock Mansion*
This restored and furnished French Renaissance-style home was built in 1914 and has 46 acres of forested and landscaped grounds.

NEAR KLAMATH FALLS: *Crater Lake National Park*
More than 6,600 years ago, volcanic Mount Mazama collapsed and formed a deep basin. Rain and snow filled it to a depth of almost 2,000 feet, creating the nation's deepest lake in a setting of rare beauty.

NEAR DAYVILLE: *Picture Gorge*
This is a basalt canyon named for the Indian pictographs on its walls. John Day Fossil Beds National Monument is also found here.

NEAR CAVE JUNCTION: *Oregon Caves National Monument*
The Siskiyou Mountains of southwestern Oregon are the site of these limestone caverns filled with beautiful formations created by the stream that runs through them.

For more information write:
THE TRAVEL INFORMATION SECTION
OREGON DEPARTMENT OF TRANSPORTATION
101 TRANSPORTATION BUILDING
SALEM, OREGON 97310

FURTHER READING

Carpenter, Allan. *Oregon*, rev. ed. Childrens Press, 1979.
Clark, Malcolm, Jr. *Eden Seekers: The Settlement of Oregon, 1818–1862*. Houghton, 1981.
Culp, Edwin D. *Oregon the Way It Was*. Caxton, 1981.
Dodds, Gordon B. *Oregon: A Bicentennial History*. Norton, 1977.
Fradin, Dennis B. *Oregon in Words and Pictures*. Childrens Press, 1980.
Thollander, Earl. *Back Roads of Oregon*. Crown, 1979.

The panoramic view from the top of the Space Needle
   in Seattle.
The deep, dark rain forest in Olympic National Park
   on the Olympic Peninsula.
Skiers gliding down the slopes in the Northern Cascade
   Mountains.
The symmetrical beauty of snow-capped Mount
   Rainier southeast of Tacoma.
The roar of the surf breaking on the rocky shore near
   the North Head Lighthouse at the mouth of the
   Columbia River.
Wide rivers floating newly felled logs to busy sawmills.

Let's Discover
Washington

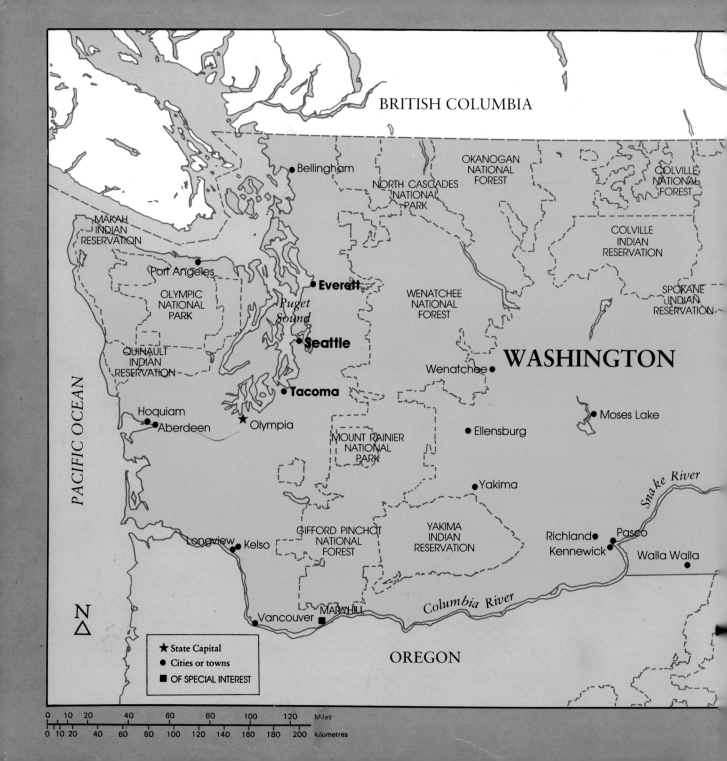

WASHINGTON

At a Glance

Capital: Olympia

State Flag

Major Crops: Grains, apples, potatoes, hay

Major Industries: Aerospace, forest products, refining, agriculture

Size: 68,192 square miles (20th largest)

Population: 4,302,000 (20th largest)

State Flower: Western Rhododendron

State Bird: Willow Goldfinch

IDAHO

Spokane

Opportunity

Pullman

Apple blossoms flower in the hills of Washington, which leads the nation in commercial apple production. The state earns more than $290,000,000 annually through the sale of fruits, nuts, and berries.

The Land

Washington is bounded on the west by the Pacific Ocean, on the north by the Canadian province of British Columbia, on the east by Idaho, and on the south by Oregon. The state has six main land areas: the Olympic Mountains, the Coast Range, the Puget Sound Lowland, the Cascade Mountains, the Columbia Plateau, and the Rocky Mountains.

The Olympic Mountains are located in the northwestern peninsula of Washington; most of the area is within Olympic National Park. Here are rugged, snow-covered mountains filled with wildlife and beautiful scenery and an unspoiled coastline still inhabited by its native Makah Indians. The main industry is logging in the mountains' foothills.

The Coast Range is in the southwestern corner of Washington. The most important industries here are logging and lumbering, but the fishing and dairy industries help support the region's economy.

The Puget Sound Lowland is located between the Olympic Mountains and the Coast Range, and extends east of these two regions to form a belt from the northern to the southern borders of the state. More than two-thirds of Washington's residents live here. It is a region of scenic and prosperous cities connected by the many arms of Puget Sound. Poultry and dairy farms and fruit orchards also flourish here.

The Cascade Mountains are east of the Puget Sound Lowland. These mountains, formed by volcanic activity, are part of a long chain that extends from British Columbia to northern California. In Washington the Cascades include Mount Rainier, the range's highest peak at 14,410 feet. In 1980 long-dormant Mount St. Helens erupted suddenly in a devastating display that spread destruction for a hundred miles around. This is a land of vast forests, mountain lakes, and glaciers. Copper, gold, and coal are mined here.

Mount St. Helens, in the Cascade Range, is one of the nation's few active volcanoes. Dormant for many years, it erupted unexpectedly in 1980, causing serious damage.

Below right:
The Columbia River, one of the state's major sources of water and hydroelectric power, forms much of Washington's southern border. Descending from Canada to flow west to the Pacific, the river is the most important in the Northwest.

Below:
The fertile soil of central and southeastern Washington is ideal for farming. In the southern coastal region, where the climate is suited to grape-growing, vineyards produce wines of excellent quality.

The Columbia Plateau covers most of central and southeastern Washington. It is a basin lying from 500 to 2,000 feet above sea level. The soil is extremely fertile, although this arid region receives little rainfall. Farmers here use irrigation to raise beef and dairy cattle, sugar beets, hops, potatoes, and fruit. The hilly Palouse country in the southeast produces most of the state's valuable wheat crop.

The steep Rocky Mountains extend through the northeast corner of Washington. This branch of the Rockies is called the Okanogan Range, and its major industry is mining—copper, gold, lead, magnesite, silver, and zinc.

Washington's coastline along the Pacific Ocean measures 157 miles, but its total shoreline is 3,026 miles, including the land along the Strait of Juan de Fuca in the northeast and vast Puget Sound with its numerous islands. The most important rivers in Washington include the Columbia, the Snake, the Colville, the Okanogan, the Chehalis, and the Cowlitz. There are many lakes in the state, some of them formed by ancient glaciation.

Western Washington, with its prevailing westerly winds and a coast washed by warm ocean currents, has a temperate marine climate, with cool summers and mild, somewhat rainy, winters. Seattle's average temperatures range from 64 degrees Fahrenheit in July to 38 degrees F. in January. On the Olympic Peninsula, just west of Seattle, the seaward slopes of the mountains have the heaviest rainfall in the United States—up to 140 inches a year. But eastern Washington has a dry, continental type of climate, with rainfall as low as 6 inches and no higher than 20 inches a year. Spokane, the chief city of eastern Washington, has an average July temperature of 74 degrees F. and an average January temperature of 25 degrees F.

Washington's total shoreline measures more than 3,000 miles, including the countless islands and coves of Puget Sound, an arm of the Pacific. The coast has many rocky cliffs and shoals that shipwrecked explorers and mariners, who named such sites as Cape Disappointment.

The History

This totem is an example of the expert woodcarving done by the coastal Indians of the Northwest and Canada, who hunted, gathered wild plants, and went to sea in large dugouts made from the region's tall trees.

Many Northwestern Indians were living in what is now Washington when European explorers arrived. East of the Cascades, in the plains and river valleys, were the Plateau Indians: the Cayuse, Colville, Nez Percé, Okinagan, Spokane, Yakima, and others. Along the coast were the Chinook, Clallam, Clatsop, Nisqually, Nooksak, and Puyallup. The coastal Indians were hunter-gatherers who depended upon fish, especially salmon, in addition to game animals. They were skilled woodcarvers, producing canoes and other utilitarian objects as well as ceremonial masks and totem poles. The Plateau Indians were hunters and gatherers who also fished in the region's streams and rivers.

In the 16th century, Spanish and English explorers skirted the coast of Washington, but the region was little known until some 200 years later. In the late 18th century, the Spaniards in California feared that the Russians in Alaska might lay claim to the Pacific Northwest, so they sent several expeditions to the territory. In 1775 Bruno Heceta and Juan Francisco de la Bodega y Quadra were the first to land in what would become Washington, near present-day Point Grenville, where they claimed the region for Spain. The British also believed that they had some title to the area after James Cook sailed along the coast and George Vancouver made a survey of Puget Sound and the Gulf of Georgia between 1792 and 1794. The United States based its claim on the explorations of Captain Robert Gray, who discovered the mouth of the Columbia River in 1792. In 1805 Meriwether Lewis and William Clark, who had been sent by President Thomas Jefferson to explore the upper Louisiana Territory and to seek a passage to the Pacific Ocean, arrived in the Columbia River country. They described southern Washington as part of the Oregon Country in the journal of their explorations, and three widely separated settlements were founded not long afterward. The

Fort Vancouver was established by Great Britain in 1825 on the Columbia River, near what is now Portland, Oregon. It was built by the Hudson's Bay Company, which had trading networks throughout the Northwest.

English established Fort Vancouver, on the Columbia, to help develop the fur trade for the Hudson's Bay Company. On the eastern side of the region, Walla Walla became a supply center for nearby gold strikes, and Presbyterian missionaries led by Marcus and Narcissa Whitman founded a mission there in 1836. Roman Catholic missionaries established a presence on Puget Sound in 1839.

Many Americans came to the Northwest in the 1840s, as the Oregon Trail opened the region to settlement. In 1846 Great Britain and the United States settled a long-standing border dispute by assigning land north of the 49th parallel to Canada and lands south of that point to the United States. The vast Oregon Territory was created in 1848 and subdivided into the Oregon and Washington Territories in 1853. At the time, the Washington Territory included not only the future state of Washington, but also northern Idaho and western Montana. In 1859 the territory was expanded to include parts of what are now southern Idaho and Wyoming. Washington's present eastern boundary was set when the Idaho Territory was established in 1863.

Mountain barriers and Indian wars deterred heavy settlement of Washington until railroad service to the East began in 1883. Over the next 10 years, the population of Washington quadrupled. Seattle became a major and increasingly cosmopolitan port—the gateway to Alaska, British Columbia, and the Far East. The Alaskan Gold Rush helped turn the city into a prosperous maritime crossroad. In 1889 Washington joined the Union as the 42nd state.

During the early 20th century, lumbering and fishing developed into important industries. Irrigation of arid eastern Washington made it possible to cultivate wheat and fruit on a large scale. Food-processing plants and canneries were built. During World War I, which the United States entered in 1917, shipbuilding became a major industry, based around Puget Sound. Aircraft construction came to the fore during World War II, and extensive dams on the Columbia River provided more electric power for industry and water for irrigation, drawing thousands of new residents to the central valley during the 1950s. The dams also fostered the development of interior ports and shipping by taming the turbulent waters of Washington's rivers.

Today, Washington is prospering through good management of its vast natural resources. It has addressed the task of diversifying its industries, many of which are highly dependent upon government contracts, especially in the aerospace field. The state attracts more visitors every year, especially since the 1962 Seattle World's Fair increased awareness of Washington's many recreational facilities. Tourism was a $3 billion business in the early 1980s. Metal products, pulp and paper, and processed foods all contribute to the state's economy.

The first school in what is now Washington opened in 1832 at Old Fort Vancouver to teach the children of those employed by the Hudson's Bay Company. Missionaries were teaching Indian children near present-day Spokane and Walla Walla in the 1830s. The statewide system of public schools was established in 1895.

Washington's first institution of higher education was Whitman College, founded in 1859. By the time that Washington became a state in 1889, there were three more—the University of Washington (1861), Gonzaga University (1887), and the University of Puget Sound (1888). Before the end of the century, 10 more colleges and universities had been established in the state.

At left:
Seattle is the largest city in Washington, with approximately 1.7 million people. It also ranks as the state's most important cultural center, with a wide variety of museums, theaters, and the nationally acclaimed Seattle Symphony Orchestra.

Below:
Bavarian dancers in traditional costume celebrate at one of Washington's international festivals. The state's many ethnic groups include Americans of Japanese, Chinese, and Philippine descent who crossed the Pacific from the Far East.

The People

Almost 74 percent of the people who live in Washington are located in urban areas, including Seattle, Tacoma, Spokane, Vancouver, and Olympia. About 90 percent of them were born in the United States, including many Americans of Oriental descent. Of the foreign-born groups, the largest are the Canadians and the Scandinavians. The largest religious membership is held by the Roman Catholics, while the Methodists and Lutherans comprise the largest Protestant groups. Other major denominations are the Baptists, Disciples of Christ, Episcopalians, Mormons, and Presbyterians.

Many prominent Americans have come from the state of Washington. Walla Walla was the birthplace of General Jonathan Wainwright, the hero of Corregidor during the Philippine Islands campaign of World War II, who was held prisoner for years by the Japanese. Well-known entertainers from the state include popular singer Harry Lillis "Bing" Crosby, who came from Tacoma, and folk singer Judy Collins, who was born in Seattle. Another distinguished native of Seattle is novelist Mary McCarthy, the author of *The Group* and other works of contemporary social satire.

Mount Rainier National Park.

OF SPECIAL INTEREST

IN SEATTLE: *Seattle Center*
Located on the site of the 1962 World's Fair, this civic and recreation center
    includes the 600-foot-high Space Needle, the Pacific Science Center, and a
    monorail to downtown Seattle.

IN WALLA WALLA: *Fort Walla Walla Museum Complex*
Here are 14 original and replica buildings from pioneer days, including a
    schoolhouse, a railroad depot, and a blacksmith's shop.

NEAR PORT ANGELES: *Olympic National Park*
The park contains 1,406 square miles of snow-cloaked peaks, glaciers, seashore,
    and rain forests.

NEAR PUYALLUP: *Mount Rainier National Park*
Dominated by mighty Mount Rainier (14,410 feet), one of the world's most
    majestic peaks, the park covers 378 square miles and is Washington's most
    popular recreation area.

IN MARYHILL: *Maryhill Castle*
An elaborate mansion built in 1926, now an art museum, this gray stone structure
    occupies a high bluff overlooking the scenic Columbia River Gorge.

For more information write:
TRAVEL DEVELOPMENT DIVISION
DEPARTMENT OF COMMERCE AND ECONOMIC DEVELOPMENT
GENERAL ADMINISTRATION BUILDING
OLYMPIA, WASHINGTON 98504

FURTHER READING

Atkeson, Ray A. *A Portrait of Washington*. Graphic Arts Center, 1980.
Avery, Mary W. *Washington: A History of the Evergreen State*, rev. ed.
    Government of Washington State, 1973.
Carpenter, Allan. *Washington*, rev. ed. Childrens Press, 1979.
Clark, Norman H. *Washington: A Bicentennial History*. Norton, 1976.
Fradin, Dennis B. *Washington in Words and Pictures*. Childrens Press, 1980.
Pellegrini, Angelo M. *Washington*. Coward, 1967.

INDEX

Numbers in italics refer to illustrations

Photo Credits/Acknowledgments

Photos on pages 5, 6–7, 9, 10, 11, 12, 16, 18, 19 (bottom left), 20 courtesy Alaska Department of Commerce & Economic Development; pages 21, 22–23, 25, 26, 27, 28, 32, 33 (top), 34 courtesy Idaho Travel Council; pages 35, 36–37, 39, 40, 41, 42, 47, 48 courtesy Oregon Office of Travel and Tourism; pages 49, 50–51, 53, 54, 55, 56, 57, 58, 59, 61, 62 courtesy Washington Office of Tourism; page 14 Library of Congress; pages 15, 30, 33 (bottom), 45 National Portrait Gallery/Smithsonian Institution; pages 19, 29 Museum of the American Indian; page 43 The Smithsonian Collection.

Cover photograph courtesy of Idaho Travel Council.

The Publisher would like to thank David W. Stewart of the Alaska Department of Commerce & Economic Development, Georgia S. Smith of the Idaho Travel Council, The Oregon Office of Travel and Tourism, The Washington Office of Tourism, and Todd DeGarmo for their gracious assistance in the preparation of this book.